The Bully

Copyright © 2024 by Shaundala Grayson
All rights reserved.

No part of this publication may be reproduced, distributed, or transmitted in any form or by any means, including photocopying, recording, or other electronic or mechanical methods, without the prior written permission of the publisher, except as permitted by U.S. copyright law. For permission requests, contact [include publisher/author contact info].

Unless otherwise indicated, all characters in this book are fictitious. Any resemblance to actual persons, living or dead, is purely coincidental. No identification with actual persons (living or deceased), places, buildings, and products is intended or should be inferred.

Book Cover by @negracomunicaciones
Illustrations by @negracomunicaciones

1st edition 2024

LESSONS IN LEADERSHIP: VOLUME 1

The Bully

SHAUNDALA GRAYSON

Author Summary

The Author has spent over 30 years working in nonprofit and for-profit companies in leadership and non-leadership positions. She now trains leaders in effective leadership geared towards progress and profit. Throughout her 30 years in both the nonprofit and for-profit arenas, she has observed and experienced various leadership styles and their effectiveness – from excellent leadership to ineffective leadership to destructive leadership.

In her career she is called on to assist companies experiencing managerial distress and to identify points of failure in compliance with laws, processes, and policies that result in employee dissatisfaction and poor bottom lines. She identifies behavioral patterns that lead to success or failure in organizations and challenges people in senior roles to self-reflect on their own leadership and managerial styles and on how they personally contribute to organizational successes and failures. She has restored employee morale in organizations on the brink of shutting down and brought them back to financial success. Her clientele includes government agencies, nonprofit and for-profit companies.

The Bully

Forward

Tales of Leadership is a collection of case studies created for anyone in a leadership position who is interested in genuine self-reflection and self-improvement that will lead to more positive and effective relationships and productivity within businesses and organizations of all types. Some will read these vignettes and be startled by the egregious behavior exhibited by some of the main characters. Others will read them and deludedly only see themselves in the more positive examples in this series, such as *The Architect or The Empowerer*. Very few will readily relate with and admit to the Serpent or the Bully within. It is that deliberate lack of self-awareness that causes leaders to miss opportunities to adjust, grow and improve the organizational climate we co-create. There is also a lesson for those of us who tolerate or ignore problematic behavior in senior leaders or understate their negative impact on the organization until it's too late.

These case studies in behavior may sound almost too bad or too good to be true, but they are all based on real people and actual events. All names and places have been changed to protect the innocent and to show some empathy for the guilty. After all, many of these leaders are not aiming purposefully to poison the environment and demotivate the people in their charge. Some of the characters are based on the combined acts of multiple people, but they are composites of no more than two people. Even then, it can be difficult to imagine that so much negative behavior can be concentrated within only two people, let alone one. To avoid naïve assumptions about what damage just one person is capable of causing to your businesses work environment, productivity, reputation and bottom line, business owners and upper level leadership would be wise to remember two sayings that ring true – "It only takes one bad apple to spoil the barrel," and "Those that don't feel embraced by the village, will burn it down to feel its warmth."

The stories in this series are meant to stimulate conversations around self and organizational improvement and will be most beneficial for those who want to analyze the success or failure of processes and checks and balances that produce leadership behaviors and hold leaders accountable. The stories are meant to be read with the intent of self-evaluation and recognizing behavior patterns that compromise your organization's health. If you read something that seems familiar within yourself or in other people with whom you work, it is because people fall into behavioral patterns that are not as unique as most people would like to believe.

For example, resorting to retribution when one feels harmed is natural. So natural and common, in fact, that laws have been put in place to protect employees from retaliatory behavior by supervisors. This urge to retaliate, coupled with the power dynamic embedded in a supervisor/subordinate relationship, can easily result in the creation of a hostile work environment. Similarly, people have a burning desire to do well. An unbalanced person with this desire, coupled with an innate lack of empathy and a supervisor/employee power dynamic, may turn into a bully who will stop at nothing to succeed, even at the expense of those they rely on for their success. The challenge posed in these writings is to be honest with yourself and acknowledge the behavior patterns into which you fall… before it is too late.

The characteristics you may see in the main characters in these tales may manifest differently in different personality types, but the stories focus on the dominant characteristic at play in individuals. For example, the Serpent certainly has characteristics of the Bully and the Puppeteer, but it is the dominant trait of emotional manipulation to "stay on top" that makes the Serpent who he is. The Bully clearly recognizes the power dynamic inherent in her position, and with a blind ambition to stay on top, she will keep others in a state of mediocracy so they will never outshine her.

Humble readers are invited to do honest self-reflection to see what traits you can discern in yourself. Readers that are able to have this deeper level of self-recognition and reflection will be able to be truly appreciate their personal contributions to the success or failure of those around them and to the projects, units, divisions and organizations they lead. A reasonable goal would be containing the Serpent or Bully within, for example, and perhaps learning to use those traits more strategically and selflessly to illicit more positive outcomes for the people you are leading or managing.

At the end of each book, there are a series of questions designed to facilitate thoughtful conversation. However, before you critique and analyze others within your organization, always first look within and ask what traits you see within yourself and, more importantly, what traits others see within you. Use these stories as a means to facilitate conversation amongst trusted coworkers and/or friends who share the same intent towards self-improvement for the individual and for the organization for which they work and which they serve.

The Bully

Contents

I am Bethany..….…… page 17

A Match Made in My Hell …………...…………..….page 27

Bullies Tend to be Short Lived, IF
You Catch Them …………………………………….page 43

What Happens Next for the Organization?…...…..page 49

Bullies Thrive Where Authority is Weak………. page 56

Notes and Conversations ……………………….... page 60

I Am Bethany

"The Earth belongs to the bullies who do not care how they get to the top, as long as they arrive."

~ SEAN PENN - Samuel J. Bicke

My name is Bethany Bullock. I live in Washington, D.C. with my 10-year-old son. I have worked for the federal government for over 25 years, working my way up from an entry level finance position to being a supervisor in the Financial Division of one of the largest agencies in the District. I credit my success to my ability to work harder than those around me, my education, my outstanding presentation skills, and my attention to detail. I have been a supervisor for seven years now. At every stage of my career, I have been promoted to the next level almost every year because of my outstanding performance. Two years ago, I was given the responsibility to manage the finances of this entire agency and supervise 30 people in the Finance Division. I am proud of my achievements because not many women make it to this level. I'm also a black woman and the agency, like many other institutions here, is white male dominated at the top. For the 18 months since I took up my role, the division has been having challenges completing tasks and projects for offices in the agency that we serve nationwide. The employees in my team need strict supervision to ensure that they are doing their jobs to a sufficiently high standard. Luckily, I am the right person for the job. I demand the highest standard of work from everyone in the division and I maintain strict discipline. I know I'm a hard taskmaster, but experience has shown me that hard work and focus are the only guarantors of success.

As of three months ago, the Agency Head placed a man called Ralph in the Financial Division over me to supervise and manage the office. Initially, I thought it was very considerate of the Agency Head to do this, because the employees under my supervision were getting out of hand. Morale and production were getting low. The rumor was that he was sent into offices to *"clean house,"* so I was glad he was here to clean out this office for me. It's really not functioning as it should.

My relationship with Ralph is a bit contentious now, but it didn't start out that way. Ralph has never worked in this area of Finance. He always asked for information from me and asked me to show him how to do things, how operations worked in the office, and how we handled assigned tasks. After a while I decided that his questions were more of a nuisance than a help, so I stopped willingly giving him information. If he was placed here, he should know the subject matter of our work. I mean, how was he going to fix the management of my office if he didn't even know Finance?

Ralph started questioning me about how I do things, and I noticed he was not focused sufficiently on the employees to find out what they were doing and ways to increase their productivity. Our relationship went from good to bad quickly and it grew more and more unsatisfactory every day. I wasn't worried about it because I knew my job. I was at the top of my game in the world of finance. He was not going to find anything wrong with my work or any gaps in my subject matter knowledge. I knew he would have questions about my staff so I let him work with them, hoping he would see for himself the ones that needed to be fired, so we really could start to *"clean house."*

Some of the people in this office have been here for 40 years or more, like Shirley, who has been here the longest and is the oldest employee in the office. She is a mid-level manager, leading a team of five people in a specialized area of the Finance Division. When the Head of the Office is out and I am not available, she is third in line and acts in the leadership position over the entire office. When I started my position, she tried to tell me how the office works, but I ignored her. She kept trying to tell me about the "working relationships" people had with one another inside and outside of the office. I could care less about who worked well with whom. All employees should be able to do what their job descriptions says, no matter who they work with. I came from another agency where I managed the office work successfully. All of our work was done, and I was recognized for my contributions on projects. I don't care about relationships among employees or about my relationship with them. I'm not here to make friends or make people *"feel good."*

One afternoon, Shirley came into my office uninvited and just sat down. She said, *"I found the lawsuits against you by your former employees you supervised before coming here. I want to help you keep that from happening here."*

I couldn't believe what I was hearing.

"Well, since you found it necessary to snoop into my background," I shot back, *"you would have seen that I won those lawsuits, and I don't need you telling me how to do my job. I mean really, if you are so good at management, why aren't you in my position? Your ways are prehistoric, Shirley, and there is no place for them under my leadership. You spend all your time worrying about what people are feeling and who is getting on well with whom, and that's why you have never moved up. The only thing upper-level management cares about is getting the work done, and they don't care how it gets done."*

Shirley looked at me earnestly, as if she was concerned about my welfare. Who did this woman think she was?

"I beg to differ!" she said. *"If you were a good manager, you would never have had seven lawsuits against you in the first place. You only "won" because the plaintiffs represented themselves and didn't know how to argue their cases without legal advice. I imagine they knew they wouldn't win those suits*

on their own, but the lawsuits were the only way they could find a voice under your leadership. That's a problem, Bethany. Don't you see that if your management skills result in so many people feeling that they have to sue you to be heard, something is wrong with YOU? I mean one or two, maybe three complaints in a person's life as a manager might be expected, but seven in two years! GIRL PLEASE! Those are shallow victories you have!"

Shirley was completely out of order. I was becoming seriously annoyed, but I know how to keep my temper and behave professionally at all times.

"Shirley, you don't know anything about me," I said, calmly and politely. *"I'm afraid you are way out of line."*

"I'm sorry," she said, in a less harsh voice. She took a deep breath. *"OK. Listen. If you do not have a good relationship with your employees, they will not get the work done that is needed for the office – and you – to be a success. And, Bethany, if you don't give your employees a voice in their work, they will take it, one*

way or another. They will be heard. It's YOUR performance evaluation that is based on these people's success, and if you piss them off, they will not work for you and your precious work will not get done. How will upper-level management view you then? They will see you as the problem."

By this point, I was infuriated by Shirley's foul-mouthed tirade. I told her, *"Anyone who does not do his or her job here will simply be fired, so they need to make a decision right now about whether they feel they have what it takes."* She knew I was talking about her.

I stood up to walk out of the office, but before I could step away, she said in a lowered voice, *"Just remember that for every action, there is an equal and opposite reaction. That goes for human relationships as well. Whatever type of energy you put into your relationships with your employees, you will get back from them."*

"This conversation is over," I said. As I walked out, I asked her to see herself out. As far as I was concerned, she was

nuts bordering on insubordinate. She had definitely crossed a line. Shirley didn't to talk to me much after that, which was good for me because she stayed out of my way.

Shirley has been here way too long and she has the other employees fooled, but not me. They really believe she cares for them, but they don't notice that the truth is that she only supports them when she is talking to them and not with her actions when they are not around. She pumps them up to their faces and sends them off to confront their mid-level supervisors when they disagree with decisions the supervisors have made, which makes them look like troublemakers. She promises she will make sure they receive promotions or recognition, but then never comes through for them. She wants them to think she has power in this office, but she has none. The employees worship the ground she walks on because she is a smart woman – a little too smart for my liking – but she has no authority to make any real decisions, though the employees don't know that.

For some reason the employees that love Shirley

overlook that she has never done anything for them when it comes time for recommendations for awards and promotions or when it's time to speak on their behalf in management meetings. Since I have been here, Shirley has never said anything to any management official to promote or support any other employee except for herself. While she is very kind to staff, she is just too lenient. She doesn't require them to set goals and meet deadlines for completing their work. And forget trying to get actual work out of her! It's next to impossible. It's just not happening. She does the minimum amount of work to meet the standards of her job description. I actually don't have a problem with that, because if she worked at her full potential, she would be a force to be reckoned with and a threat to me in this office. I gladly allow Shirley to work in mediocrity so that she won't outshine me.

**

A Match Made In My Hell

Three months ago, just before Ralph came to the division, upper-level management hired some new staff. I wasn't a part of the hiring process, but I did get a chance to review the new employees' resumes once they were hired. The most experienced by far was Michael. He had a lot of private sector experience and had been doing this work for over 35 years. He has two degrees in our area of finance, and it was clear he is very well respected by his peers. He came with outstanding references. He was even able to train and mentor some of the employees who already worked for us on new approaches and practices in our work area. Our paths had crossed many years ago when he had even trained me in this area of work at another job site. He truly understood the work. I found him to be an excellent trainer and I knew he had excellent supervisory skills. He could do every job in this office exceptionally well, including mine. Which was a worry.

I asked Michael why he was here, given his background. He said he wanted to slow down and not take on management responsibilities at this stage of his career and this job allowed him more freedom in his personal life. I was relieved with his response. He wouldn't be competing with me.

We also took on a woman called Lisa, who was a younger employee. When Ralph arrived, he really seemed to take to her. He said she reminded him of his daughter, and that he felt she had a lot of potential. He wanted to mentor her to make sure she had a successful start in her career in this area of finance and he really took her under his wing. I personally didn't see the potential in her and I certainly didn't believe that his investing time in her was good for accomplishing the goals for the office. I found her very difficult to work with because she seemed to only do what Ralph wanted her to do and she ignored my directives. I was finding Ralph more and more obstructive and not the kind of help I imagined he might be when he was first assigned to the division.

Ralph asked Michael to work with a member of the team named Vera, to see if he could help her improve her area of work, which was about providing financial guidance to management in other offices in the country. Vera has worked at the agency for over 30 years and was close to retirement.

Vera, like me, wasn't originally from America and was a woman of color. English was not her first language, and she certainly didn't speak *"the King's English"*. I found it embarrassing when she spoke: splitting verbs, mispronouncing words. Oh, my god! It's mortifying to be around her when she is speaking. I myself was born and raised in England and I am proud of my English accent and the looks I get when I speak to people. People here are surprised when they hear a woman of color speak with an English accent.

I don't even think that Vera has a college education. I am really surprised that despite her lack of education, most of the offices that reach out to this office for assistance ask for her. I don't understand what help she could possibly provide to them – a woman who can't even put together a proper sentence with a subject, agreeing verb, and without using dangling modifiers. Let's not even talk about her writing skills.

When Ralph assigned Michael to work with her, it was

like mixing oil and water. I couldn't see how they would possibly work together. On top of all of his experience outside of this agency, Michael had impeccable writing skills. He had even authored articles on his areas of expertise in finance. I thought Ralph did it to put a buffer between Vera and the rest of the employees in the agency. I really didn't think it was a good match because they were so vastly different. I knew Michael wouldn't like this assignment. Vera was so beneath him in education and presentation skills.

One day when I called into the office looking for Vera, I was told that she wasn't there. She had taken Michael to other offices in the building to introduce him to colleagues whom our office serves. When he came back to the office, I asked Michael how it went. I was surprised when he told me that Vera had a vast amount of knowledge about the agency and its mission. Most importantly, according to him, she knew all the key people in the agency. He said she had introduced him to leadership in the General Counsel's Office, Contracting, and even in the Agency Secretary's Office. I hadn't even had these introductions, and I wasn't pleased about that. He said all of the employees that he met embraced her with such fondness and loved her dearly. Michael also told me that it was mainly because of Vera's relationships with all of the employees in the agency and her extensive institutional knowledge that she was able to get a lot of work accomplished under her area goals for the office. I noticed that most of the time when people came to the office, they bypassed me and went looking for her. I just assumed it was because I hadn't been here as long as she had. I never understood why they looked for her. I thought maybe they were coming to complain about her work with them, even though I never received a complaint. I couldn't believe that someone with such bad communication skills could be sought after for business advice, especially more than me.

None of this mattered to me because as far as I was concerned in terms of her contribution to the office, her verbal and written communication skills left so much to be desired, she would never be able to make a useful contribution. I asked Michael what improvements he could make in Vera's area, which, I reminded him, was why Ralph had assigned him to work with her. He said he was able to assist her in certain areas of written policy, best practices, and guidance for other employees to follow. Ralph was very pleased with the outcome. They were both awarded for their work, which came as a complete surprise to me because Vera couldn't complete a proper sentence as far as I was concerned.

One day, Vera was sent on an assignment to another office and she left without telling me. Several employees were sent on this assignment by upper-level management, and when this happens managers, such as myself, have no control over where or when employees leave. However, out of respect, she should have told me. I didn't like the fact that she left without giving me notice. I wanted to teach her a lesson and make sure she understood her place in this office. I told Michael I was going *"get her"* for doing that. I felt Michael was someone I could confide in, since he wasn't competing for my job.

When Vera returned, I was more diligent about watching her time and attendance and I provided her with much more critical feedback on her work product. There was just so much wrong with her work that needed to be brought to her attention in her performance evaluations. She turned in a report summarizing the people that she and Michael served at the agency, and I believed that it was so full of inaccuracies. I told Michael that her work product was not good enough and he actually challenged me! He asked me, his supervisor, to show him where the errors were in her work. I didn't dignify his request with a response. He continued to defend Vera, at which point I deemed their relationship as *"unhealthy."* I told Ralph they should be separated. Ralph refused to separate them, saying that work productivity in their area had increased by 65% with them working together. I simply don't believe him. Fortunately, I have power over Michael's performance evaluation so I knew I could get him to be compliant by marking him down in areas of his performance to make him change his behavior.

One day I was working from home, as I did three or four days out of each week. I emailed Michael and told him I wanted a meeting with him and Vera. He didn't respond to my email. I emailed Vera and she also didn't respond. I sent them each at least 10 emails that day and neither one responded. I was so angry, I decided to call on the phone at the end of the day to confront them for ignoring me. Michael picked up and said that they hadn't had a chance to check emails because of the influx of work they had from clients. I told Michael it was obvious they couldn't manage their time, so I was putting Suzette over them as a Team Leader. I pulled Suzette from a different Team handling a different area in Finance in the office. She had some experience in what Michael and Vera did but nowhere near the level of experience they had. She would not outshine me in managing them, but she always does exactly what I tell her to do. Michael asked me why I would do that because Suzette had such little experience in his and Vera's area of work. Again, how dare he question my decisions! I told him that Suzette clearly respects me. I told her to watch over them and let me know when they arrived at work, when they left the office, how long they took for lunch and anything else she could that would give me ammunition to write them up when they slipped up. I was determined show them who is boss. Suzette did all that I asked. Michael and Vera couldn't stand her. They had a horrible relationship with her, but I wanted them to understand their position under my supervision. Michael and Vera weren't to do anything unless I told them to, and I would rate them accordingly to keep them in their places.

Vera complained about me to Ralph, claiming I was harassing her and that I was creating a hostile work environment for her. I told Ralph that I was just doing what her other supervisors should have done long before I came along to correct her mistakes and give her the performance rating she deserved. After she complained about me, I immediately moved her from her work area and placed her in another area in which she hadn't previously worked. She and Michael were finally separated. Michael's performance went down, because he was not processing the same number of cases as he had been with Vera, and he told Ralph he *"missed Vera"*. I laughed at the notion. Vera's outstanding performance went down because she was in the new area that she was not familiar with. I had them where I wanted them. I think Michael just thought too much of himself. He thought he was better than me. I showed him who was boss by giving him a poor performance evaluation because he was not producing the same number of cases as he had been with Vera.

Vera was sent on another detail by upper-level

management and, again, she didn't tell me about it. She had the nerve to tell me that when the details come from upper-level management, employees don't have to tell their supervisors anything. She even showed me the handbook in which this policy was written. I told her I didn't care about that policy because I had never worked at an agency where an employee didn't have to tell her supervisor when she was going to be gone. I disregarded this agency policy and I didn't care. I was going to use what I could against Vera. I wrote her up for being insubordinate and I wanted her fired. With Suzette's help, I created a paper trail to get rid of Vera. She was not going to outsmart me in any way whatsoever, and she certainly was not going to outshine me in this office.

About 30 days went by and Vera submitted a reasonable accommodation with documentation from her doctor requesting that she work from home five days a week due to mental disability of anxiety and depression. Her job was undeniably 100% teleworkable. I told her she had to provide more details from her doctor. She provided additional information, but the doctor's note looked suspicious to me. I called the doctor's office and asked the doctor if she actually wrote the note. I told the doctor she did not have to lie for Vera. The doctor confirmed that she wrote the note, but I still didn't believe it. I requested that she provide Vera's medical file to me. The Doctor refused.

Vera's performance went further down. She submitted an appeal for the denial of her accommodation request and I denied it, telling her that her current performance didn't allow her to work from home and I was still waiting for further documentation from her doctor. She said she was waiting for her doctor to respond, and she asked me specifically what was missing in the documentation. I told her: *"Your doctor has to sign every page on the packet of forms I gave you."* She responded,

"There is no place for the doctor to sign on each page, only the last."

"Your doctor did not provide a diagnosis on this particular page."

"There is no diagnosis requested on that page."

"OK then, your responses are sufficient. You don't need to provide any more documentation."

I denied her request again because her doctor had not signed each page or provided a diagnosis on the correct page. I told her to do it again. She said, *"My relationship with my doctor is very strained right now because of your requests. She is not going to provide any more documentation for this request. I don't understand why you are not granting my accommodation request. I am so miserable in this office. I am making my coworkers unhappy because I cry all the time."*

"You have to come in here just like everyone else. I expect you to be here tomorrow at 8:00 a.m."

"I have a standing appointment with my therapist tomorrow."

"Then 8:00 a.m. the next day."

"I have an appointment with my primary care physician. Can you please give me two or three dates that

I can choose from, so I can coordinate with my doctors' treatment schedule?"

I refused to respond. Vera sent me 15 emails asking me to give her dates to respond. I felt that was harassing. I told her she was abusing me with her emails and I was not going to stand for it. I refused to respond, and she was not to work from home until I gave her permission. I was going to get rid of her. She had to come into the office every day just like everyone else whether she had a disability or not. She started taking a lot of sick leave for doctor visits and I constantly reminded her by email that she had to be able to do her work with or without an accommodation.

Vera was pulling the morale down for the office. Work productivity was much lower than it was when I first started. It was all because of Vera and Michael. Sick leave taken by all employees was at a record high. I discovered that someone had even anonymously filed a complaint about the office, causing an investigation to be conducted, which is what had led to Ralph being sent in to *"clean house"* and get the employees in their place and back on track. The rumor was that it was Suzette that filed the complaint! I was floored when I heard this. I mean, after all I had done for her! I confronted her about this, and she said she resented me using her to do my *"dirty work."* I was shocked. I told her I was mentoring her on how to be a good manager.

My relationship with Ralph was still frosty. I avoided him whenever I could and he seemed to spend all his time *"helping"* employees, which was not what he had been sent in to do. His job was to get everyone back in line. The fact that they obviously needed his help just proved they were not up to the job.

As I said earlier, the new arrival, Lisa, became a favorite of Ralph's. Lisa was Ralph's pet. He gave her every possible opportunity to shine. He took her on office visits and gave her opportunities to train other employees across the agency that he should have been giving to me. He allowed her a lot of opportunities that I never had when I was her age. I had to scratch my way up to my position and no one ever gave me such a helping hand. At one point, I learned that he was allowing her to telework on a project for the same number of days per week that I was teleworking. It made me mad to see her getting the same privileges as me when she clearly didn't deserve it. I had to admit that her work product was excellent. I didn't want her to move up, so she also had to be put in her place – back down to the level of the mediocrity of all the other employees in the office. I refused to give her an excellent appraisal. She deserved an average rating because she needed to work as hard as I had to work at her age. Rating her as excellent would just make her more full of herself than she already was. Also, there was no way she was going to get a rating higher than my rating in this office.

* * *

Bullies Tend To Be Short Lived, IF You Catch Them

A few days later, it was time for Bethany's annual appraisal, which was carried out by Ralph. People outside the closed door of Ralph's office looked at each other wide-eyed as they heard the unmistakable sound of Bethany crying inside the office. After half an hour or so, she emerged red-eyed and walked quickly out of the room with her head down, looking at no one.

Ralph had been assigned to the department to discover why performance and productivity had slumped. After his first interactions with Bethany, his subsequent conversations with members of the team and many weeks of watching Bethany's behavior towards the people she supervised, it became obvious to him that Bethany was a workplace bully and the source of the department's problems.

In his appraisal of her, Ralph had given Bethany a truly dreadful performance rating. Bethany had been genuinely shocked. She burst into tears and begged Ralph not to do this to her; she had never received a poor performance rating before in her career. Ralph did not remove Bethany's status as supervisor, but he moved her to a desk in the middle of the floor with the rest of the employees. He also moved Bethany's things out of her office and placed two employee's desks in the office, saying that they *"needed the space."* Then, his task completed, he left the office.

Bethany seemed to learn nothing from the episode. She discounted everything Ralph had told her about her behavior – what did he know? – and convinced herself that she would be promoted to Ralph's position now that he was gone. She would be able to explain the poor performance rating Ralph had given her: the man clearly had some personal animosity towards her; her performance was just as strong as ever. She looked forward to getting her revenge once she was promoted. She was certainly going to get all the people who had crossed her. They were going to be very sorry they had stirred things up. They had clearly lied to Ralph about her and tried to blame her for their own poor performance and lack of ability. She hated working at a desk alongside the other employees, but she sensed they were all still frightened of her. They were terrified about what she would do when she was in an even more powerful position. They were right to be terrified, Bethany thought to herself with grim satisfaction.

But Bethany was not promoted into Ralph's vacated role. The agency hired an outsider, a lady called Ruth, to take over Ralph's role. Bethany was stunned. She couldn't believe it. It took her several days to get over the shock, but then she began the process of educating Ruth as to what was really going on in the office. Ruth had probably got the wrong impression about her from Ralph's report. Bethany assumed that Ralph had told all kinds of lies about her. She cozied up to Ruth and began to tell her the "real truth" about people in the office, especially Vera, Michael, Suzette and Shirley. Vera was still pretending she was ill. Michael's performance had fallen way down. Suzette had proved herself to be a snake in the grass and Shirley – well, Shirley was just out of touch and obsessed with "working relationships". She never did any real, useful work. Lisa was still a threat, of course. Bethany went out of her way to explain to Ruth why she had not been able to give Lisa a good performance rating and that Ralph, quite frankly, obviously had a soft spot for Lisa and thought she could do no wrong.

One day, Bethany sent a particularly harsh email to Michael, picking him up on some supposed issue with his work. Michael replied and copied Ruth into his reply. In his response, he told Bethany what an appalling supervisor she was, citing several instances of her unfair criticisms and bullying behavior. At the end of the email, he said that he was handing in his notice.

As news of Michael's resignation spread around the office in the coming weeks, several more employees followed suit and resigned. The full extent of the damage done by Bethany's bullying became clear. Ralph had taken action to take Bethany down a notch and make her seem less powerful in the office, but more drastic action was clearly needed. Ruth demoted Bethany, removed all employees from her supervision, and told her she would never supervise another person at the agency while Ruth was the manager. Bethany left the agency less than a year later. Nevertheless, she was able to move to a role supervising staff at another agency, explaining away her demotion as being the consequence of a departmental restructuring and pointing to her impressive career performance.

The Bully

* * *

What Happens Next For The Organization/Business?

Bethany, like the other characters in this series of vignettes about bad behavior in the workplace, is fictitious – but her character is an amalgam of several real workplace bullies that the author has encountered. Bullying in the workplace is shockingly common. The 2021 Workplace Bullying Survey by the Workplace Bullying Institute (WBI) showed that 49% of all Americans had experienced past or present bullying at work, with 30% who have had direct bullying experiences and 19% who had witnessed bullying at work. This equates to 79.3 million Americans with experience of bullying at work.

Workplace bullying can take many forms, but includes unreasonable work demands; shouting and yelling at staff; threatening people, overtly or covertly, with the loss of their jobs; criticizing their abilities; insulting them or running them down, privately or publicly; discounting or denying their achievements; taking credit for their work; and deliberately excluding them from various activities to make them feel unwanted and not a full member of the team.

Bethany's favored bullying technique is to actively prevent people from working to their full potential so that no one can outshine her, and to use her power over people's performance ratings to keep them in line and hold back their careers. Bethany is not physically or emotionally capable of developing positive human relationships. When she feels disrespected, she goes after people via their performance ratings and through disciplinary actions. She separates employees when they find synergy with one another to get the job done well because she sees that as "ganging up against her," especially when they do something differently than she would, even though they get the same or a better result. She has little tolerance for those with a lesser education than she has. She seeks to maintain control by any means necessary. She destroys people mentally and emotionally just to let them know who is boss, and that is satisfying to her. Her bullying attitude means that the people in her department are demotivated, cowed, under- supported and under-appreciated, while her vindictive streak adds an extra dimension of real fear that Bethany might "write them down," leading to blocked routes to promotion and even dismissal.

Bethany's lack of self-awareness is not unique, but it is unusual. Many bullies are, at least to some extent, aware of their bullying behavior. Some are natural bullies; some have come to believe that bullying works for them at work; others see bullying as entirely appropriate "management" behavior. In the 2021 WBI survey, 4% of respondents self-identified as bullies – a horrifying 6.6 million Americans who are aware of their buying behavior at work.

Bethany is aware that she sees people as threats and takes action to neutralize them, but she is completely unaware of the overall impact of her behavior on her division. She is aware of her own strengths and abilities, knowing that she has always been highly successful in her career to date. She believes she is continuing to operate effectively in her role as a supervisor, without any understanding of the extreme negative impact of her bullying management style on her team's performance.

For any organization, the Bethanies of this world are extremely expensive. To say that they "fail to bring out the best in their teams" massively understates the real damage they do. They actively destroy the potential of their teams and create hostile environments that make people stressed, unhappy and unproductive. Bullies can go undetected for a long time because people are frightened to speak out against them. In Bethany's case, the rapidly deteriorating performance of her department caused alarm bells to ring, leading to Ralph's appointment to try to find out what was going wrong. He correctly identified Bethany's behavior as the root cause of the problem and took steps to make her seem less domineering by moving her to sit among her colleagues. Unfortunately, it was not until Michael's resignation and the testimony he supplied about Bethany's behavior that the full extent of the damage she was causing to the office became clear. Subsequent resignations by colleagues who had been suffering under Bethany's reign of terror but now felt empowered to follow Michael's example confirmed this.

It can be very difficult for employees to challenge a bullying boss when they are not certain they will be supported by senior management. Bullies are often very good at forging excellent relationships with senior management and persuading them that their "challenging" behavior is essential and productive. People reporting to

Bethany could not be certain that senior management had not been similarly persuaded and that they might take Bethany's side in a dispute. After Michael's resignation, other colleagues decided to do what they had been considering for some time and leave the agency. Bethany had been allowed to get away with her bullying behavior for too long; people had lost faith in the agency's ability to prevent any future bullying.

Bethany's lack of self-awareness meant that she was unaware of senior management's and her immediate colleagues' perception of her behavior. She genuinely believed she was taking effective action to "control" the people under her supervision. She presented herself to senior management as a highly effective manager. She readily admitted that she was a "tough" boss who demanded the highest standards of work – something senior managers were, in principle, quite comfortable with. Senior management had failed to pick up on the many clear indications that Bethany was a bully, not a "tough" manager.

Even after Michael's resignation and Bethany's

demotion, she began immediately to rationalize events, persuading herself that people were just "out to get her" and that she had done nothing wrong. Ralph had been appointed to investigate the division only when its declining productivity made it clear there was something wrong with the way the department was being run.

* * *

Bullies thrive where authority is weak

- Tim Field

There is no easy solution for organizations that discover a bully in their midst. It is feasible, but very difficult, to change a bully's behavior through the disciplinary process. When bullies realize that their behavior is not secretly condoned or even welcomed by senior management – something many bullies persuade themselves to be the case – they might come to realize that they need to radically reassess their behavior in order to progress within the organization. But many bullies are incapable of real, fundamental change. Once you notice a person's bullying behavior at work, you will likely notice that it manifests in every aspect of their life: someone who is a bully at work is also a bully in the community, in the church, and at home. There is also nothing "personal" in the relationship between a bully and their targets; they will bully anyone and everyone if they are able; some people, like Michael, just prove more resistant to their bullying tactics than others. But even his resistance had limits. His resignation caused great loss to the company of a person who had skill and talent that that Division needed, even more than it needed Bethany.

Organizations are not in the business of psychotherapy;

it is highly unlikely that the organization will be able to fundamentally change a bully's approach to life through internal disciplinary action and coaching.

If you discover a bully in your organization, here are a few questions you might like to ask yourself about the consequences the organization has experienced since you hired this person:

- Have incidents of sick leave increased?
- Have more people left the organization than would be usual?
- Are fewer people being commended in general or being put forward for promotion – does it seem as if talent is not being recognized?
- Has the number of people receiving bad appraisals increased?
- Have there been formal and informal complaints against the person concerned?
- What is the general atmosphere like at work: do people seem happy, fulfilled, and motivated, or anxious, stressed and cowed?

The answers may give you cause for concern. If they do, look the facts in the face. The bully may seem to be effective; they may have an impressive track record as an operator – though almost certainly not as a manager. They will have a compelling story to tell you about how wonderful they are and how the things you may have heard about them are malicious gossip started by people who are not good at their jobs but whom the bully has uncovered and is now beginning to scrutinize.

Step back, look at the facts, and ask yourself which version of reality is correct.

Notes & Conversations

Notes

What traits of The Bully do I recognize in myself?

Notes

Ask your coworker/friend what traits of The Bully does s/he recognize in you?

Notes

Ask people under your leadership what traits of The Bully do they recognize in you.

Notes

What can I do to lessen the negative traits identified within myself?

Notes

What parts of The Bully's traits do I believe I need to be successful?

Notes

What traits of The Bully have I experienced in others at work, religious organizations, nonprofit organizations, and other organizations in which I give my time and work with others?

Notes

How have people with The Bully's traits affected the environment(s) in which I work or volunteer my time?

Notes

How do we work together to eliminate The Bully within ourselves and others in order to be successful together in the work that we are doing?

Notes

How do I believe The Bully became a bully?

Notes

Is it possible for me to empathize with The Bully? If so, how, and would it affect the way I relate to her or him?

Notes

Do I recognize some of these traits in people from my childhood or in children with whom I work?

Notes

Notes

Notes

Notes

www.ingramcontent.com/pod-product-compliance
Lightning Source LLC
Chambersburg PA
CBHW050014230526
45470CB00003B/957